QUARTER-MIDGET
RACING is for me

QUARTER-MIDGET RACING
is for me

Mark Lerner

photographs by
Robert L. Wolfe

Lerner Publications Company   Minneapolis

The author would like to thank Matt Cole; Ardyth, Kevin, and Kurt Belker; and all of the members of the Minnesota Quarter-Midget Racing Association for their help in doing this book.

To the Big D

LIBRARY OF CONGRESS CATALOGING IN PUBLICATION DATA

Lerner, Mark.
  Quarter-midget racing is for me.

  (Sports for me books)
  SUMMARY: Matt describes the technical, organizational, and strategical aspects of his first quarter-midget race.

  1. Karting—Juvenile literature. 2. Karts (Midget cars) —Juvenile literature. [1. Karting. 2. Karts (Midget cars)] I. Wolfe, Robert L. II. Title. III. Series.

  GV1029.5.L47   796.7′6   81-41
  ISBN 0-8225-1125-8

Manufactured in the United States of America

International Standard Book Number: 0-8225-1125-8
Library of Congress Catalog Card Number: 81-41

1 2 3 4 5 6 7 8 9 10 90 89 88 87 86 85 84 83 82 81

Hi! My name is Matt, and I like to race cars. The cars I race are not real ones, though. They're **quarter-midget cars**. They are called quarter-midget cars because they are about one-fourth the size of real race cars.

The actual size of quarter-midget cars is regulated by strict rules. The cars can be no more than 80 inches long, and they must have a **wheelbase** between 42 and 52 inches. The wheelbase is the distance from the middle of the front tires to the middle of the rear tires.

Quarter-midget cars cannot be more than 28 inches high. This does not include the **roll cage**, the bars above the driver. The roll cage prevents the car from falling on the driver if the car happens to flip over.

I've been driving for only a short time. My brother Brad has raced for over a year, though. He's pretty good. It was Brad who got me interested in the sport. I liked to go to the track to watch Brad race.

My friend Kurt also races. His older brother, Kevin, is his **handler**. A handler is like a coach. All quarter-midget drivers have adult handlers.

One day I was watching Brad and Kurt race, and Kevin asked me if I would like to try racing. I said that I would love to! Kevin said he would be my handler. I took my first drive the following Sunday before the day's races started.

I used Kurt's car to take a few practice laps around the track. Twenty times around made a mile. Here's a drawing of a typical quarter-midget track. It's oval shaped.

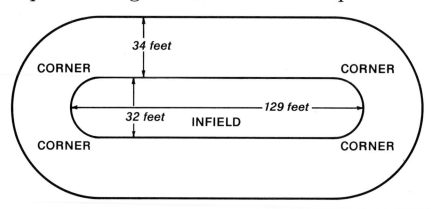

I liked driving very much. It felt good to be behind the wheel. I couldn't wait to actually start racing. Kevin thought that I would be ready to race the next week.

Now it was time for Kurt to race. At first he did very well. But then he had car problems. During the final race of the day, Kurt's engine "blew." It made a loud bang and stopped running. Kevin couldn't fix the engine at the racetrack, so Kurt couldn't race anymore that day.

After the races, I went back to Kurt and Kevin's house. We went to Kevin's workshop and took the engine out of the car. Then Kevin opened the engine and looked inside. No wonder it had blown! The **piston** inside the engine had exploded. The piston is a very important part of an engine. When the piston moves up and down, it makes the power that drives the car's rear wheels.

Taking apart the engine was fun. I learned a lot by watching Kevin and asking him questions. He's a good mechanic, as all handlers should be. Kevin put a different piston into the engine and said that the engine was now as good as new.

During the week, I couldn't stop thinking about my first race. Kevin told me that I would be racing in the **senior novice class**. Novice classes are for beginners. Senior drivers are between 9 and 15 years old. Last year, when I was 8, I would have raced as a **junior novice**. That class is for beginners who are between 5 and 8 years old.

Four other classes would race on the same day that I did. These classes were **junior stock**, **senior stock**, **modified stock**, and **B-modified**. Stock drivers must use engines that have not been changed in any way. The engines must be just like they were when they came from the factory. Modified engines, though, may have some changes on them.

The two most competitive classes are the modified stock and the B-modified classes. The drivers in these classes use engines that are more powerful than the ones used in the other classes. The modified engines have **carburetors** that let in more air and gas than stock engines do. The more air and gas that an engine burns, the faster it can run.

Kurt drives in B-modified races and senior stock races. Drivers may compete in two classes, but not more. There is no novice class for modified stock or B-modified races. So while I'm still a novice, I can race in only one class.

As soon as I've had enough experience as a novice, I will race in the senior stock class. Drivers must compete in at least three novice races before they can qualify for the stock classes. The handlers decide when drivers can advance from the novice class to the stock classes.

The day of my first race finally came. It had rained during the night, and the sky was still cloudy. When Kevin and I got to the track, we saw that it was wet and very slippery. At first it looked like we wouldn't be able to race.

Before anyone could take a practice drive around the track, the handlers got together to decide if we should race or go home. I was happy when they decided to hold the races.

Before the races could begin, though, we had to dry off the track. We did this by taking turns driving on it. We didn't drive too fast. We just warmed up our engines and let the exhaust and the friction of our tires on the track dry it.

When the track was dry, we were ready to begin. A quarter-midget competition includes two **time trials** and three separate races.

The time trials are first. Each time trial is one **lap**. A lap is once around the track. The first race is called the **heat**. It is 10 laps. The second race is the **semi**. It is 15 laps. The third and final race is the **feature**. The feature is the most important race of the day. It is 25 laps.

In each of the three races and in the better of the two time trials, drivers earn points. The higher a driver finishes, the more points the driver gets. The heat and semi are each worth 10 points to the winner. The second place finisher gets 9 points, the third place finisher gets 8 points, and so on. The winners of the feature and the time trials get 20 points each. Here are the points you can get for each race:

TIME TRIAL:		HEAT	
Finishing Position:	*Points:*	*Finishing Position:*	*Points:*
1st	20	1st	10
2nd	18	2nd	9
3rd	16	3rd	8
4th	14	4th	7
5th	12	5th	6
6th	11	6th	5
7th	10	7th	4
8th	9	8th	3
9th	8	9th	2
10th	7	10th	1

SEMI:		FEATURE:	
Finishing Position:	*Points:*	*Finishing Position:*	*Points:*
1st	10	1st	20
2nd	9	2nd	18
3rd	8	3rd	16
4th	7	4th	14
5th	6	5th	12
6th	5	6th	11
7th	4	7th	10
8th	3	8th	9
9th	2	9th	8
10th	1	10th	7

At the end of the feature, the drivers' points from all of the races are added together. The driver with the most points is the winner. Each class has one winner.

A driver's performance in the time trials determines where the driver will line up at the start of the heat race. In a time trial, drivers race against the clock. They are timed twice, and the better time is recorded.

When it was my turn to be timed, Kevin pushed me from the **staging area** to the **hot chute**. Drivers and handlers work on their cars in the staging area. The hot chute is the place where drivers start their engines and get ready to enter the track.

Kevin pushed me out of the hot chute and onto the track. I took five warm-up laps. Then I got the green flag. This is the signal that the clock has started. The green flag is just one of several flag signals used on a racetrack. I had to learn what all the flags meant before I could race. Kevin had tested me, and I had passed. Here's what each flag means:

COLOR	MEANING
Green	*The race has started.*
Green ⎰ *waved* *Yellow* ⎱ *together*	*Line up properly to* *begin the race.*
Red	*Stop your car* *immediately.*
Black	*You are disqualified.* *Leave the track.*
White	*One lap left in the race*
Checkered	*The end of the race*

When I got the green flag, I drove as fast as I could. It seemed that I finished the lap in no time at all. At the end of the lap, the flagman waved a white flag. That meant I could take one more practice lap before my second time trial.

After this warm-up lap, I got the green flag again. So I drove my second timed lap. My engine sounded smooth. I could feel it pushing hard behind me. I knew I would have a fast time. Then I saw the flagman wave the checkered flag to end my second time trial.

Kevin went to the scorekeepers, who were sitting above the track. They told him what my times were. Only my faster time would count. My second lap was better. It took only 7.6 seconds. Wow! That was fast, and I felt great.

After the time trials, I drove to the weighing area. There a scale weighs each car. In some classes, drivers are also weighed. My car passed the weigh in. That meant I was eligible to compete in the races. Sometimes cars and drivers are not the right weight. Then they are disqualified and cannot race.

I waited and watched while the other drivers finished their time trials. Jeanette was the last senior novice driver to finish. Her time was fast, and her faster lap took only 7.8 seconds. My time was the best of all in our class, though. So I won 20 points.

When the time trials for all of the classes were over, we were ready for the heat race. I found out my **grid** position. The grid is the lineup at the beginning of a race. The grid for the heat race was in the **inverted** order of the time trial finish. That meant that the fastest drivers would be at the back of the grid. So Jeanette and I lined up in the back row.

The handlers pushed their drivers out of the hot chute, and we began to take our warm-up laps. The flagman waved two rolled-up flags. One was green, and the other was yellow. That was our signal to get into the grid position. When the flagman saw that we were all in the right order, he waved the green flag to begin the race.

Right away, Jeanette cut in front of me. She was quick. I tried to cut in front of another driver, but I couldn't. He had beat me to the corner. He turned the corner closer to the grass than I did. So I couldn't get inside like I had wanted to.

Four, five, six laps passed. I was still in last place. Then I made my move. I used the **slingshot pass**, which Kevin had taught me. To make a slingshot pass, you have to get right behind the rear bumper of the driver you want to pass. Then when the driver turns and heads toward the outside wall, you cut inside and put your car between the other car and the grass.

The slingshot pass moved me into fourth place. I felt ready to move ahead even more. But then, with only three laps left, something in the back of my car started to slow me down. I knew there was a problem. My back wheels were not spinning smoothly. With only two laps to go, I had to drive off the track.

Kevin helped me pull the car into the staging area. There we checked to see what had made the car slow down. Kevin saw that my **drive tire** had slid into the **torsion bar**. The drive tire is the back tire that is connected to the engine by a chain.

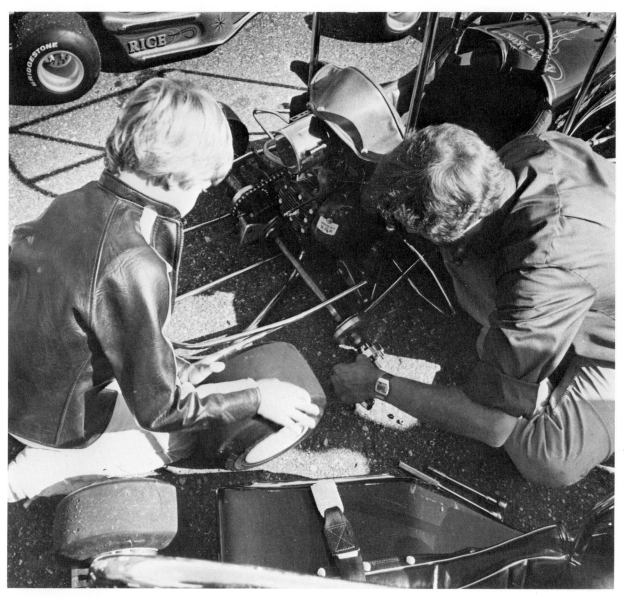

When the engine's power moves the chain, it turns the drive tire. That action moves the car. The torsion bars are shock absorbers. They keep the car steady as the car rides over bumps. Kevin and I replaced the drive tire and the other rear tire with new ones.

Between the heat and the semi, Kevin and I went to eat lunch. We bought hot dogs and soft drinks at the concession stand. Everybody at the track goes there to eat and to talk between racing events.

Kevin said that in the semi I should "ride the wall" on the straightaways and turn the corners close to the grass. He said that if I didn't cut toward the grass on the corners, my car would spin out. Riding the wall means getting as close to the wall as you can. When you're close to the wall, you can drive faster than if you stay next to the grass.

The grid for the semi was not inverted.
Drivers were positioned in the same order
that they had finished the time trials. So
this time the best drivers in the time trials
lined up at the front. The blackboard showed
my car, Number 61, right in front.

I started the semi in first place, but I knew it would be tough to hold the lead for 15 laps. The race began okay, but soon I got into trouble. On the 5th lap, a driver passed me with a slingshot pass. Then another driver passed me. At the end of the race, I was in fourth place. Jeanette won.

Kevin cheered me up after the race. He said that I just needed more experience. It wasn't easy to drive right behind cars and then pass them. I knew learning how to do that well would take time.

The last race of the day was the feature. If there were no accidents, the race would be over in about three and one-half minutes. I lined up near the front of the grid because I had not won many points in the first two races. Jeanette had the most points, so she lined up at the back.

In the feature, I held the front position for 8 laps. I was driving very well when suddenly I saw the flagman wave the red flag. I stopped my car and looked behind me. Two cars had collided.

Fortunately, neither driver was hurt. That's because all drivers are very well protected. We wear helmets, jackets, and gloves. Each car must have a strong metal frame. And safety belts must be worn at all times. It's good to know that my favorite sport is very safe, even if accidents sometimes do happen.

The cars that had collided were damaged, so the drivers had to leave the race. When the feature started again, I was in second place behind Jeanette. The two drivers behind me tried very hard to pass me. But I drove close to the grass on the turns, and I didn't let them pass. I held on to second place as the race ended.

When the total points were counted, I finished second in my class. That made me very happy, because it was only my first race. Jeanette had the most points, so she was the winner. Jeanette is a good driver, and she deserved to win.

It was getting dark, so Kevin and I put our equipment away. Another handler helped Kevin lift my car onto the trailer. Now we were ready to go home. It had been a fun day. And now I can hardly wait until next Sunday when I race again. Quarter-midget racing is *really* for me!

Words about RACING

CARBURETOR: The part of an engine that mixes the gas and the air needed to power a car

DRIVE TIRE: The rear tire of a car that is attached by a chain to the engine. The drive tire pushes the car.

FEATURE: The last racing event of the day. The feature is worth more points than any of the other races and is 25 laps long.

GRID: The lineup, or positions, of the cars at the start of a race

HANDLER: A driver's coach and mechanic. A handler must be at least 16 years old.

HEAT RACE: The first competitive race of the day. The heat is usually 10 laps long.

HOT CHUTE: The area where the cars are started before being pushed onto the track

INVERTED: In reverse order. In an inverted grid, the best drivers from the previous race line up at the back.

JUNIOR: Classes for drivers between 5 and 8 years old

LAP: One complete drive around the track

MODIFIED: Classes for engines that have been changed in some way

PISTON: The part of an engine that moves up and down and powers the chain attached to the drive tire

ROLL CAGE: The bars above the seat that protect the driver if the car should flip over

SEMI: The second competitive race of the day. It is usually 15 laps long.

SENIOR: Classes for drivers between 9 and 15 years old

SLINGSHOT PASS: A method of passing a car by driving close to its rear bumper and then sharply cutting inside it toward the grass

STAGING AREA: The place behind the track where handlers and drivers work on their cars before the races

STOCK: Classes for engines that have not been modified

TIME TRIAL: A race against the clock. A driver's finish in the time trials determines where he or she will be positioned in the grid for the heat race.

TORSION BAR: The shock absorbers that keep the car steady as it rides over bumps